Quick
&
easy

Hermit
Crab
Care

T.F.H. Publications
One TFH Plaza
Third and Union Avenues
Neptune City, NJ 07753

This book has been published with the intent to provide accurate and authoritative information in regard to the subject matter within. While every precaution has been taken in preparation of this book, the publisher and author assume no responsibility for errors or omissions. Neither is any liability assumed for damages resulting from the use of the information herein.

ISBN 0-7938-1014-0

www.tfh.com

Table of Contents

What is a Hermit Crab?

Hermit crabs are interesting, clean, and easy-to-care-for animals. They can be found in many pet stores and even in small gift shops along the beach. Land hermits are kept by thousands of people, young and old alike.

This book will provide you with the necessary care, feeding, and housing information that will help you enjoy your pet to the fullest.

Hermit crabs (also known as hermit tree crabs and soldier crabs) are crustaceans, belonging to the class Crustacea, as do blue crabs, shrimp, and lobsters, among other groups. There are several different families of hermit crabs and hundreds of species. Authorities differ as to the exact taxonomic placement of land hermit crabs within their class. Some lump them on the family level with other hermit crabs and some give them a family status of their own. For the purposes of this book, we'll consider land hermit crabs as members of the family Coenobitidae, which has two genera, *Birgus* and *Coenobita*.

The unique Coconut or Robber Crab, *Birgus latro,* is a fully terrestrial hermit crab that doesn't need to carry around a snail shell to protect itself. These crabs may be a foot in length and six pounds or more in weight. They are found in tropical mountains and along shorelines from eastern Africa to the South Pacific. Coconut Crabs are usually brown to blackish in color, and their claws are sometimes white. Unlike other hermit crabs, they have four symmetrical pairs of walking legs. These crabs do not appear for sale in the hobby and are almost never imported.

All the land hermit crab species look much alike. This specimen is from Northern Territory, Australia.

Quick & Easy Hermit Crab Care

The most familiar land hermit crab is the Caribbean, Coenobita clypeatus. *This specimen is from Venezuela.*

There are several species in the genus *Coenobita*, which is the type of land hermit usually sold as a pet. The most common is *Coenobita clypeatus*. Individuals of this species are easily obtained on the Caribbean islands and in southern Florida. Its distribution is strictly tropical, and these crabs are seldom found more than a mile from the ocean.

Stop!

The temptation to pick up a land hermit crab or two the next time you are vacationing in southern Florida is strong, but ecologically isn't very sound. Too many tourists, vast changes in the beaches of southern Florida, and the fact that these crabs are near the northern edge of their geographic range all are combining to reduce the number of land hermit crabs in southern Florida.

What is a Hermit Crab?

A trio of Caribbean land hermits grazing on a lawn at night in southern Florida. This species is easy to take care of and long-lived.

Other species in this genus include *Coenobita compressus, C. rugosus,* and *C. perlatus* (the latter called the Strawberry Land Hermit). These species are all found near shorelines of the Indian and Pacific Oceans and seldom are available as pets.

Name Game

It is interesting to note that the name "hermit" as applied to these crabs is misleading. In the wild, they live in groups and may travel in large packs, roaming the shorelines at night in search of food. The "hermit" label actually refers to the solitary existence of the crab in the shell it takes as its home.

In their natural environment, land hermit crabs have been known to migrate in large numbers over long distances, but they generally stay within a hundred yards of the shoreline. They can be found almost anywhere from sandy beaches to the tops of small trees and steep cliffs. These crabs are not aggressive, and crabs of many sizes are often found living together. In most cases the crabs seem to ignore each other. If one encounters another crab in its travels, it will climb over it as if it were just an empty shell.

Ecologically Important

Land hermit crabs are important as scavengers along almost all tropical shorelines. They recycle everything from whales to mangrove leaves and pandanus fruits. Few predators feed on them, however, and they are relatively long-lived, which means they may reach gigantic numbers in suitable areas.

Structure

Land hermit crabs are decapods; that is, they have ten legs. The first pair of legs, called the chelipeds, ends in claws (pincers) that are different from each other. The left leg has a large pincer, called the

The legs of a land hermit are compressed (flattened) and curved to help the crab tightly close the opening of the shell when it withdraws.

chela, that is used for climbing and defense. This chela is purplish in color in the Caribbean Land Hermit. The enlarged pincer also serves to block the opening to the shell when the crab withdraws. By blocking the shell, the crab not only protects itself from predators, but it helps conserve moisture within the shell. The smaller, right pincer is generally an orange to brownish color and is used for eating and climbing. The second and third pairs of legs are called ambulatory (walking) legs. They are the four legs that the crab uses to walk. The fourth and fifth pairs of legs never extend out of the shell under usual circumstances and are used by the crab to hold itself inside the shell and to maneuver the shell while walking. Land hermits have a long, curved abdomen that allows them to fit into the curled interior of a snail shell.

Shell Legs

In hermit crabs the last two pairs of legs (number four and five) are very short, asymmetrical, and have roughened areas on their edges. They function to help hold the crab in its shell and not to help the crab walk, though they technically are still called "walking legs."

Hermit crabs have two major sections to their body, like other related crustaceans. The front part is the cephalothorax, with the head area fused to the thorax. The eyes, antennae, and mouthparts are at the front end of the cephalothorax (the head), which is marked by a thickened area called the shield. The gills and the walking legs are under the back part of the cephalothorax. The rest of the crab's body is the abdomen, which has only a few traces of the wide chitinous bands (segments) that mark the abdomen of a shrimp or lobster. In hermit crabs the small legs (pleopods) of the abdomen are reduced in size or absent to allow the hermit to more easily slip into and out of a snail shell.

The gigantic purple claw (on its left front leg) is a great defensive feature of the Caribbean land hermit and also helps ensure a moist shell.

What is a Hermit Crab?

Antennae

Like other crustaceans, land hermit crabs have two pairs of antennae. The outer pair is long, while the inner pair (antennulae) is shorter, flattened, and ends in flattened sensory segments. Land hermits find their food largely by smell, the antennae being their most important sensory organ.

The hermit crab's eyestalks generally are flattened from side to side (compressed), and the long stalk-like projections between the eyes (the bases or peduncles of the two pairs of antennae) have compressed filaments at the ends. The antennules are hinged at their bases and can be moved up and down and to the sides to orient to scents. Land hermit crabs are very sensitive to vibrations in the soil and have poor eyesight.

Although crustaceans use gills to breathe, land hermit crabs have gills of reduced size because the cephalothorax is narrow compared to typical crabs. In fact, the undersurface of the abdomen has thin

Aggression

A land hermit crab sometimes communicates by using a whirring-chirping sound. These noises have been heard during aggressive encounters in the crab's native environment and are seldom heard in captivity. The only observed aggressive behavior has been when one crab will shake or rock another to drive it from a shell that the aggressor wants. Even in this act, neither crab is harmed. Of course, a soft, recently molted crab might be considered as food and attacked and eaten, but this is not truly aggressive behavior—unless you are the soft crab.

patches with blood sinuses under the skin. These patches and sinuses function like gills by utilizing the air carried in the small

Head Shield

Scientists long have found hermit crabs difficult to study because they are asymmetrical animals, their left and right sides not being identical (or sometimes even similar). How do you even measure the length of such an animal? Scientists who study hermit crabs measure the shield, the thickened, usually saddle-shaped area behind the eyes that has a strongly curved border. A hermit crab with a shield length of 5 mm (fifth of an inch) might have a cephalothorax over an inch long and a total length of 3 inches or more.

amounts of water held in the crab's shell. This storage supply of water allows a land hermit crab to travel far from the ocean and carry its breathing water with it.

Except for the Coconut Crab and a few others, hermit crabs have twisted, nearly naked abdomens with a reduced number of small leg-like appendages (pleopods) compared to typical shrimp, lobsters, and crabs. Females usually have three pleopods on the left

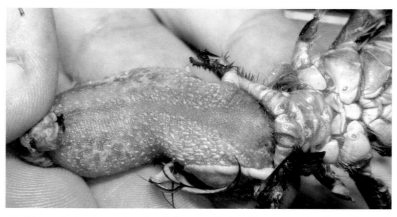

A thin, naked strip under the abdomen of a land hermit crab allows the crab to absorb extra air from moisture in its shell.

What is a Hermit Crab?

side of the abdomen in land hermits, but these are absent or almost invisible in males. Loss of appendages is related to adaptations for holding onto the snail shell the hermit uses for cover.

Choosing a Pet Hermit

When purchasing a land hermit crab from a pet store, choose one that is the size you want, is active, and looks healthy. Check to see that it has all its legs and grasping claws. Depending on the size of the crab, you may want to purchase one or two extra shells at this time so your crab can switch shells when it feels like it. Some crabs are more colorful than others, probably due at least in part to diet and age, but those you see for sale probably will all be the same species, *Coenobita clypeatus*, the Caribbean Land Hermit (though some dealers may have a few Eastern Pacific Land Hermits, *Coenobita compressus*). The smallest you encounter will hardly be larger than a pea, and the largest might have a truly gigantic claw and inhabit a 10-inch conch shell.

When you are buying your crab or crabs, try to pick up the proper terrarium at the same time. Buying the substrate and a tight-fitting

Getting Started

Once you've decided that you want a pet hermit crab (or several) be sure to bring home everything your new pet will need, including:

- adequately-sized plastic terrarium with a secure lid
- substrate (such as sand)
- things for your crab to explore and play on (such as rocks, empty flower pots, coral)
- water and food dishes
- hermit crab food
- extra shells

Most pet shops carry a vast assortment of hermit crab supplies.

Your hermit crab must have more than one shell to be happy. Be sure to always purchase a few extra shells of the right size and opening shape.

cover now also makes sense, as does picking up some crab food to tide you over until you get into the feeding routine.

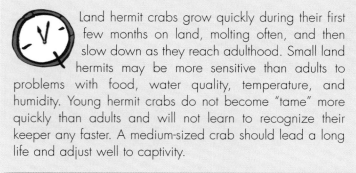

Size

Land hermit crabs grow quickly during their first few months on land, molting often, and then slow down as they reach adulthood. Small land hermits may be more sensitive than adults to problems with food, water quality, temperature, and humidity. Young hermit crabs do not become "tame" more quickly than adults and will not learn to recognize their keeper any faster. A medium-sized crab should lead a long life and adjust well to captivity.

Land hermit crabs make good pets, as they are easy to care for and have very simple requirements. Even though these animals are relatively inexpensive to purchase and maintain, they should not be considered "throw away" pets. They deserve the best keeping conditions you can provide for them. All land hermit crabs are collected from the wild, so each one that dies is a loss from nature.

Quick & Easy Hermit Crab Care

Shells, Molting
& Handling

The land hermit crab's shell is not really its own. The crab actually lives inside a discarded snail shell. After mating, the females carry fertile eggs to the sea and release them into the water. From this point on, growth is rapid and the crab eventually develops and crawls ashore. The young crab instinctively searches for an empty shell and claims it for its first home. The search for a more suitable home will never stop. Each shell the crab happens upon will be examined, first to see if it is occupied, then for suitability as to its size, cleanliness, and weight. If things look good from the outside, the crab may try the shell on. The transfer to a new shell is made rather quickly, because the crab is extremely vulnerable outside the shell. The crab may even switch back and forth between the old shell and the new shell until it decides which one it prefers. This search continues for the rest of its life.

Shell Choices

In nature, land hermit crabs do seem to have favorites when it comes to choosing a good shell. They can quickly evaluate the shape of the opening and the fit of the abdomen inside the shell, as well as the weight of the shell. A crab may try on several shells before finding the perfect fit.

Extra shells should always be available for your crabs, both for their enjoyment and for potential new homes as they grow. Additional shells may be purchased where you bought the crab, or you may

Some keepers like brightly dyed shells for their crabs, others like them natural. The crab in this fluorescent shell won't really care.

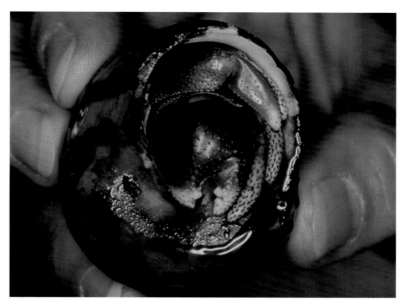

As long as the shell fits the crab and allows it to close up easily and move around, your crab will not care whether its shell is red or green, smooth or spiny.

collect shells from the seashore if you have the opportunity. Be sure to select shells that have a somewhat circular opening and are at least as large as the shell your crab is currently occupying, preferably a little larger. Before putting a new shell in the crab's enclosure, soak it overnight in fresh water to remove any chemicals or residues that may be harmful to your pet.

Shell Limits

The availability of suitable shells on a beach may limit the number of land hermit crabs found there. Simply put, if the crabs can't find the right shell to give them protection and free movement, they look elsewhere until suitable shells can be found. This means that the distribution of land hermit crabs along the shoreline of an island is not uniform, because the different types of snails also are not evenly distributed.

Never try to remove or force a crab from its shell. A land hermit will allow itself to be torn apart at the junction of the cephalothorax and abdomen rather than leave its home and its protection. Even if you just pull at it a bit, its claws and legs may break off, stressing the crab and making it difficult for it to feed and walk. Lost appendages usually are replaced with smaller versions at the next molt.

Incidentally, land hermits are not found just in snail shells. The shape of the opening is more important than the external appearance, and as long as the abdomen fits comfortably and is protected, a crab will use what is available. Sometimes land hermits are found in shotgun shells, rifle cartridges, light bulb bases, perfume bottles, and coconut shells. They often use fossil shells where these are available.

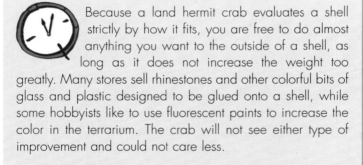

Decorations

Because a land hermit crab evaluates a shell strictly by how it fits, you are free to do almost anything you want to the outside of a shell, as long as it does not increase the weight too greatly. Many stores sell rhinestones and other colorful bits of glass and plastic designed to be glued onto a shell, while some hobbyists like to use fluorescent paints to increase the color in the terrarium. The crab will not see either type of improvement and could not care less.

Caribbean Land Hermits living in Bermuda at the northern edge of the range face a special problem when it comes to finding shells to use. In much of the Caribbean these crabs prefer to use the conical black-and-white streaked shell of a large turban snail known as *Cittarium* (formerly *Livonia*) *pica*, the West Indian Top Shell. This snail seems to have the perfect combination of opening size and shape, shell weight, and strength, as well as abundance, to be a favorite. Unfortunately, this snail became extinct in Bermuda

Though they would seem hard to maneuver, larger land hermit crabs do well in spiny murex shells. Again, the size and shape of the opening are most important in shell selection.

Shells, Molting & Handling 21

several thousand years ago, though the land hermits continued on. There are no fresh, living *Cittarium* shells on Bermuda for the crabs to use, but there are scads of fossils available in deposits at higher elevations on the island. These have been dug out by the hermit crabs, cleaned off, and then used just as if they were from freshly dead snails. The shells are passed back and forth generation after generation, and the crabs carry them to all parts of the island. Few other large snails are common in Bermuda, and the crabs actually need these fossils to continue their abundance on the island. Visitors to Bermuda often consider *Cittarium pica* to be one of the most abundant animals because the shells are found everywhere, including gardens and in cities, and in all sizes, but every one of these shells seen is a fossil, dug up and utilized by a land hermit trying to find just the right shell.

There are many accounts of great shell-trading conventions that took place under the eyes of impartial and objective scientific observers. The crabs may congregate on a beach or other open area,

A hermit crab holds itself in its shell with the short fourth and fifth pairs of legs, which you will seldom see.

When a land hermit crab gets ready to change shells, it can move very fast. Its abdomen is soft and curved and is easily injured when exposed.

and for several days thousands of land hermits swap shells back and forth and perhaps engage in some mating as well. One observation of such an event on Mona Island off Puerto Rico 50 years ago reported that tens of thousands of Caribbean Land Hermits climbed down the cliffs and marched to the beaches, where they remained for several days, swapping shells, climbing trees, and probably mating.

Land hermits will use any shells with an opening suitable to house their abdomen and not too heavy to move around comfortably. They especially like West Indian Top Shells (*Cittarium pica*), many other round-mouthed top and turban shells (turbos), whelks, crown conchs (*Melongena*), star shells, common rock or dye shells (*Drupa, Thais,* etc.), babylon tops (*Babylonia*), murex shells of various types, and smaller conch shells (*Strombus*) that are not too heavy. Shells with narrow mouths such as cone shells and cowries just don't fit over the abdomen correctly. On islands or isolated coasts where

Shells, Molting & Handling

suitable snails may not be especially diverse or common, shells often are passed around from crab to crab over generations until the interior supporting structure of the snail shell is actually worn away.

Because hermit crabs pay little attention to the outside of the shell, adding decorations such as fake jewels and metallic paint (as long as it is waterproof) does not hurt. Some keepers like the look of natural shells, while others think that the more jewels that have been added the better the shell looks. Smaller land hermits will use colorful land shells of the right size and shape, such as candy-striped tree snails.

In addition to the shells of dead land and sea snails, an excellent source of empty snail shells for growing hermit crabs is from other growing hermit crabs. A small crab finds an empty oversized shell and moves into it since it is better than what he had. A larger crab in an undersized shell meets that smaller crab in the oversized shell and a trade is accomplished. Sometimes the two crabs seem to come to a mutual agreement to trade, but more often the larger crab asserts itself and the greater force prevails. In hermit crabs, size determines dominance, so the larger crab always wins.

Molting

The crab's real shell or exoskeleton does not grow as the soft tissues under it grow. Land hermit crabs actually grow by shedding their exoskeleton. A new exoskeleton is constantly being developed underneath the old one. Every few months (depending on temperature, food supply, and age) the old exoskeleton will be molted or shed and then discarded or eaten. During this molting period the crab will grow back any missing legs (though they may be smaller) and probably look for a place to hide. The crab may decide to burrow into the substrate of its cage during molting because it is defenseless at this time and is quite vulnerable to predators; it also dries out quickly. If your crab is hiding, it should not be disturbed, and it might be better to remove other crabs from

Molting Dangers

Because the muscles of a hermit crab fasten to the inside of the thick exoskeleton, it follows that if the exoskeleton is soft the animal cannot move correctly because the muscles will not be able to exert sufficient pressure. Chemical salts in the exoskeleton of a newly molted crab must harden by exposure to air for hours or days before the shell is strong enough to allow proper muscle pull. Until then, a molted "soft" crab is easy prey for other hermit crabs and must hide.

its terrarium for a week or two. The new exoskeleton will fully harden in five to ten days.

Handling

Small crabs are easily handled and can be trained to eat while in your hand. Keep your fingers together with an outstretched palm

Many hermit crabs will peacefully walk on your hand. Be sure there is a soft surface under them in case they fall, however. Some hermits are pinchers and will not allow handling.

As with any pet, it is not a good idea to leave a young child with a land her-mit. The child might try to pull the crab out of its shell (resulting in damag-ing the crab) or might be pinched (which is painful but actually harmless).

and place the crab on it with some food. If you do this every day, the crab will become accustomed to handling. Remember that the crab's pincers are used for climbing, so if it decides to climb off your hand it may use the pincer to hold on. If you do get pinched,

Hermit Crabs and Small Children

A large land hermit crab has an extremely powerful left claw with strong muscles. The front leg also is very maneuverable, so the crab can reach well back over its shell with its claw. Small children should not be allowed to handle large hermit crabs because, simply, they will be "bitten" (pinched), and the pinch is very painful and may draw blood. Also, the crab often does not want to let go, adding to the terror a child might feel in such a situation.

Quick & Easy Hermit Crab Care

Look at the fingers of the big claw of a Caribbean land hermit. Now visualize the muscles inside this claw. Can you understand why being pinched can be so painful?

remember that the crab is not trying to hurt you, but just trying to hold on and keep from falling. Avoid putting your crab in a position where it feels insecure or has the possibility of being dropped.

Some crabs may be quite defensive at first, and their pinch can be very painful, even drawing a bit of blood. They also do not like to let go. If you just try to pull the crab off you will break off the pincer, which may retain its hold on you even then. If your pet crab has latched onto you and refuses to let go, you can hold it under running luke-warm water for a few seconds. This will not hurt the crab. It usually is better to run the water over the back of the shell, thus over the crab's abdomen, which is more delicate than its head end.

Exercise

You can let your crab get some exercise and roam the floor or wander around a room as long as you are there to watch it. Avoid letting a dog or cat near a roaming hermit crab, as trouble is sure to follow. Remember that land hermits can climb well.

Quick & Easy Hermit Crab Care

Housing & Feeding

Keeping a land hermit crab is really simple. Feed your pet as much as it will eat. Remove uneaten food before it spoils. Provide fresh, clean water in a shallow container that is easy for the crab to enter and leave. Avoid slippery bottoms and tippy or deep bowls; your crab might actually drown if it cannot get out of its water dish.

Basic Care

Land hermit crabs enjoy temperatures in the range of 75 to 80°F, so they are comfortable in most homes. Extremes beyond 90°F should be avoided. At low temperatures they become dormant and may die when below 60°F; at high temperatures they try to burrow into

Nocturnal Wanderers

Though land hermit crabs may be found active at any hour, they really come out to feed and play at night. In nature the day is spent hidden under leaves and other litter or in burrows, sometimes many yards from the sea. At night the crabs leave their hiding places and venture to the shore to eat and replenish their water supply. This cycle also occurs in the terrarium.

moist, cool sand or sit in their water bowl. Land hermit crabs have no additional heating or lighting requirements, though it is best to not place them in direct sunlight. Keep the crab's home away from radiators and air conditioners, as this will rapidly change the temperature in the crab's cage. Your crabs will be most active at night, but expect some activity during the day as well.

In nature and in the terrarium, land hermit crabs are most active at night. This means they will feed best after the lights go off.

Quick & Easy Hermit Crab Care

A simple aquarium with the right substrate, some climbing branches, and a sturdy cover to help conserve moisture and prevent escapes can serve as home for several young and adult land hermits.

Keeping a relatively high humidity in the terrarium is very important for the health of the crab. Try to hold the humidity to about 60%; purchase an inexpensive humidity gauge (hygrometer) to help you keep things constant. The inside of the terrarium should not be damp all the time, and the bottom should not be moist all the way to the surface. Instead, try to provide a bottom that is nearly dry at the top and becomes wetter as the crab would burrow down into it.

Terraria

The best housing for land hermit crabs is a glass or plastic aquarium. Smaller crabs can be kept in a very large fish bowl (too little bottom area for comfort, however), but larger crabs should be kept in an aquarium ranging from 10 to 15 gallons, depending on the number of crabs you are keeping as pets. The crabs get along well with each other, though each will develop its own personality. As many as 10 adult crabs can be comfortably housed in a 10-gallon aquarium, but of course fewer crabs will create less mess. The size of their home

Housing & Feeding 31

will depend on the amount of space you have available to set aside for them in your home.

Plastic carriers with vented plastic lids work well and are light and fairly tough. They are high enough to allow you to add sufficient substrate and even a climbing branch or two, yet still give one or two crabs enough area to roam and exercise. Hermits often like to climb to the lid and then hang upside down.

Plastic!

Plastic carriers make excellent cages for one or two hermit crabs or as temporary housing for larger numbers. They are easy to clean, tough, look good, and come with vented lids that are generally secure enough to hold in even large hermits. If the humidity drops in the carrier, try putting a sheet of plastic over part of the opening and then holding it in place with the lid. The light weight of plastic carriers is a great advantage when dealing with heavy substrates and large animals housed in heavy shells.

Be sure to put a lid on the terrarium so the crabs do not climb out and escape and so you can control the humidity. A sheet of glass or plastic is the best type of lid, though if you cover the entire surface of the terrarium with it you will get condensation that may be harmful and lead to growth of fungus. If you are keeping larger crabs, the cover should be fastened in place with lid clamps or weighted down to help prevent escapes.

Substrate

The substrate for the terrarium can be anything from sand to aquarium gravel to potting soil. The depth should be 1 to 3 inches. If you are not adding live plants to the terrarium, you may wish to use a cleaner, easily handled bottom material such as sand (which can be made to stay moist during molting periods) or gravel. Most keepers prefer to use a bottom of crushed coral, coral rock, crushed clam and oyster shells, or limestone. Crabs kept on pure silica sand don't do as well as those that have access to calcium-rich substrates, which probably give them an additional source of calcium for their exoskeletons.

Sand

Calcium sands are perhaps the best type of substrate for a land hermit crab, with gravel a bit less desirable. Crabs often burrow into the substrate after molting, using it both as a hiding place and a place to keep moist, and sand is excellent for this. If possible, try to keep the top of the sand relatively dry, adding water in the corners so the sand near the bottom of the tank stays moist.

Crabs like to climb (in the wild some have been found in trees) and need exercise, so you should add different objects for the crab to explore and climb on such as rocks, coral, driftwood, and ceramic ornaments. Remember that land hermits are agile and curious animals and prone to escape. Be sure that the distance from the tip of the highest point they can climb to the top of the cage is more than twice the height of the crab and its shell. You also should realize that crabs can form bridges by climbing on each other's backs, making it possible to reach points much further from the bottom than you might think. You may also want to include a few hiding places in the tank to be used after molting.

Cleanliness

The crab's terrarium should be cleaned thoroughly at least once a month. If you are using gravel, remove all the substrate, rinse it

Climbers

Land hermit crabs have been called tree crabs, and they definitely do climb well. They use the walking legs with their sharp tips to scuttle up low bushes, while the snail shell provides protection if they fall off the bush. In the terrarium most land hermits will use a piece of driftwood for climbing, often bunching up at the end of the highest branch.

well (DO NOT USE SOAP), and let it dry before you return it to the tank. If you are using sand as a substrate, replace it monthly. This will prevent feces and uneaten food from accumulating in the cage. Every few days check the terrarium for waste matter, bits of food, and general dirt. Some keepers suggest rinsing off a crab and its shell in clean water each week just to

Small land hermit crabs can serve as living decorations on sturdy branches and bits of driftwood in the terrarium. Their pointed legs and strong claws give them a sure grip.

Though fresh water works well for the Caribbean land hermit, other species may require salt water. It might be best to offer two bowls of water, fresh and salt.

make sure food residues do not become trapped in the shell, there is at least some water for the crab's gills, and the shell stays clean and bright.

Water

Hermit crabs prefer moist environments. You can keep the terrarium moist by misting the crabs with moderately warm water a few times each week. Crabs are known to become more active after being misted. Never submerge your crabs for any length of time. These are land crabs, and they could drown. Keeping a shallow bowl of water in the terrarium allows the crab to moisten its gills on a regular basis and add some water to its shell for trips into dry areas. Though these are marine crabs, most seem to do just as well with clean fresh water as with salt water, and few hobbyists bother adding any salt to their water. However, you might want to play safe by providing not only a dish of fresh water but also one of salt water. A solution of about an ounce of table salt (non-iodized) or

Fresh Water Only?

Land hermit crabs are all marine animals, so their metabolism is based on drinking salt water. In the terrarium, however, keepers have found that Caribbean Land Hermits do about as well with fresh water, and indeed in nature some crabs are found along freshwater streams away from the beach. Though it does not hurt to provide both fresh and salt water, as long as the water is clean and chemically safe there should be no problem with any water given to Caribbean Land Hermits.

commercial sea salts to a quart of water can be tried. Some land hermits, such as the Eastern Pacific Land Hermit, come from areas with little fresh water and are adapted to drink and use only salt water.

Illnesses

There are not many hermit crab diseases you can cure or control except by proper nutrition and hygiene. Lost legs will be regenerated eventually. Undersized shells should be exchanged for larger ones to accommodate growth. Damaged shells should be replaced promptly for protection of soft parts from both parasites and dehydration. There are some parasitic mites that may be found

Chlorine

Not all water is equal. Chlorine is used to treat human water supplies and may combine with other chemicals (such as ammonia) to produce even more complicated chemicals deadly to crabs. Use bottled water if you have any doubts about the purity of your tap water. Water conditioners used for marine aquaria also have been successfully used with land hermit crabs.

Regeneration

The biggest problem you will have with your crab is occasional accidents resulting in losing a leg or claw. If fed well and kept at the right temperature and humidity, the crab should regenerate a replacement leg with the next molt. However, new legs and claws tend to be smaller than the originals and often not as colorful. It may take several molts to fully repair a lost leg.

on your hermit crab, but they usually are tiny, difficult to see, and hard to remove; some live only in the gills, where you would never find them.

Feeding

Feeding land hermit crabs is easy. They are omnivores, which means they will eat almost anything. In the wild they are scavengers. A

Though land hermit crabs are scavengers, they enjoy a good salad with a nice mix of greens and chopped fruits on occasion. Use salads to supplement pre-pared foods.

In a Pinch

If your pet shop does not have hermit crab food and you don't feel like raiding your refrigerator for suitable leftovers, try giving the crabs turtle food. The pelleted turtle and tortoise foods sold by most pet shops are based on a variety of ingredients, all readily accepted by hermit crabs. You may have to lightly moisten larger pellets; if so, remove uneaten scraps before they fungus.

good, commercially-prepared hermit crab food should be a regular part of their diet. Most pet shops that sell land hermits also sell food for them.

Crabs also like bread, crackers, lettuce, apples and other fruits, coconut, grapes, oatmeal, cornmeal, dry dog food, and dry scraps of fish and chicken. An occasional treat of a little peanut butter is okay. A few bits of shrimp (with the shell) will supply carotene, which helps a crab retain its reddish colors. Frankly, almost anything may be eaten. Crabs find their food mostly by smell, tracking the scents with their antennae.

Calcium

It is important for land hermit crabs to get calcium in some form, either through a calcium powder supplement added to their food, a cuttlebone to chew, crushed oyster shell, or boiled, crushed eggshells. The calcium will boost the metabolism of the crab and produce stronger exoskeletons after each molt. Many crabs eat their shed skeletons to regain the calcium from it.

Don't forget that your pets need calcium in their diet. Calcium can be gotten from the coral sands of the substrate, but it helps to add a supplement to their food or give little bits of cuttlebone regularly.

If you keep several hermit crabs in one terrarium, be aware that a molting hermit is very soft and defenseless and might be considered food by its companions; this is why molting crabs hide or burrow into the moist substrate. Land hermit crabs are scavengers, after all, so any weakened animal is a potential food item.

When feeding the crabs, be sure to remove uneaten fresh foods (fruits and vegetables) after a day, so they don't spoil. Don't worry if it seems as though your crabs are not eating—they can go for long periods without food, though of course they should always have food provided for them daily.

Quick & Easy Hermit Crab Care

Breeding

L and hermit crabs are faced with several problems not shared by most other animals. For instance, they must find empty snail shells of the appropriate size as they continue to grow through their long lives. Also, the females must get their eggs to seawater even if they live a mile inland.

There is a lot we don't yet know about breeding and life cycles in land hermit crabs, but the basics are pretty well understood. It seems certain that when the ancestors of the land hermits left the sea, they didn't really leave it entirely. The adults still return for a dip or a drink from time to time, and the eggs will not develop anywhere except in seawater.

Because of how they are kept, land hermit crabs do not reproduce in captivity. There have been occasions when female crabs carrying eggs were caught on the way to the water to release their eggs. When placed in a terrarium with access to seawater, hatchlings were obtained. These were maintained by feeding them brine shrimp larvae as the crabs went through the several developmental stages (larvae) leading to the tiny final stage crab that leaves the water and resembles the adult.

Sexes

Reliable sex determination can be made only when the hermit crab is removed far enough from its shell so the bases of the legs can be seen. Male hermit crabs have a pair of enlarged pores at the bases of their fifth legs, sometimes with a curved projection extending from the base of each leg. Females have flattened, membranous disks at the bases of their third legs. Females usually have three small pleopods (false legs) on the side of the abdomen; these are absent in

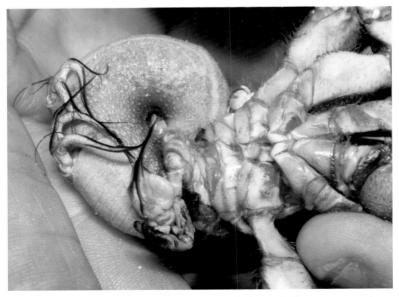

This ventral view of a female land hermit crab shows the large pores on the basal segments (coxae) of the third pair of walking legs. Males lack these pores but have pores on the fifth coxae.

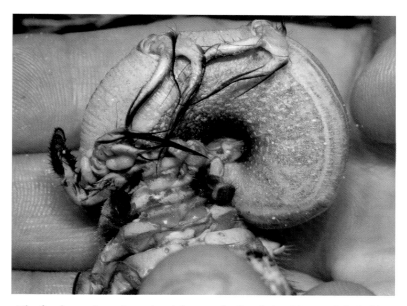

The few large pleopods on the abdomen of a female land hermit help hold the eggs under the abdomen until they are deposited in the sea.

males. Aside from this, there are no obvious external sexual differences between male and female land hermit crabs.

Mating

Unlike many crustaceans (including the familiar freshwater crayfishes), mating is accomplished on land and the female does not have to be freshly molted in order to accept sperm from the male.

Claw Size

In many crustaceans males have larger claws than females. This is because a male must maneuver the female into place for successful mating, using his claws, and males also often are competitive when looking for females. As far as known, in land hermits there is little aggression between males, and females are very cooperative when mating. Perhaps for these reasons claw sizes in land hermits of both sexes are similar.

The color, size, and shape of the large claw of Caribbean land hermit crabs do not vary with the sex of the crab. Other factors, genetic and environmental, cause the claw to vary a bit.

Males find females, possibly by smell and possibly by touch, and the pair maneuver their bodies and shells together until the male's fifth legs are near her third legs. Packets of sperm are passed from the male to the belly of the female, where they fertilize eggs coming from the bases of the third legs. The eggs find their way onto the surface of the female's abdomen, where they hang on special hairs and leg-like processes.

Later the female wends her way to the shore where there is true salt water of high salinity. She hangs onto mangrove roots, stones, and debris at the edge of the water and drops her eggs into the water. Adult hermit crabs swim poorly or not at all, thus they tend to avoid entering deep water. If the water is too deep to safely tip her body into the water, she may literally propel the eggs into the water from a short distance and a safe perch.

Quick & Easy Hermit Crab Care

Larval Development

Shortly after they enter the water, the eggs hatch and the first larvae of the hermit crab emerge. These are called the zoeal stage and are symmetrical and shrimp-like, with eyes on short bases. The zoea grow and metamorphose through four or more zoeal stages over the course of several weeks. They then molt into the next stage, the megalops, which looks much like a normal crab with a long,

When a land hermit crab moves onto the land, it finds a tiny shell that will fit it. The rest of its life is spent moving to larger and larger shells as it grows.

symmetrical abdomen and large eyes on long stalks. After this stage they become more hermit-crab like, the abdomen becoming asymmetrical with reduced appendages and the body taking form. This last group of stages, called the glaucothoe stage, continues with slight changes after each molt until the young hermit crab looks much like the adult and leaves the water to find its first snail shell on a damp beach or the edge of a brackish or freshwater pond. The interval from egg to tiny crab varies greatly with temperature and season, but several weeks are required at a minimum.

Age

Females can start laying eggs when they are about the size of the first joint of your thumb, about two years old. At that time they may produce perhaps a thousand eggs. As they grow older and larger, they lay more and more eggs, up to perhaps 50,000 eggs at a mating. Obviously most of the larvae don't make it, or the ocean shores should be literally buried in land hermit crabs. Once they make it to the beach, a land hermit crab can live at least 10 to 12 years, perhaps longer. In captivity, a few keepers have had land hermit crabs survive for over 20 years.

Death

Though land hermits may live a decade, most pets probably live only a year or two. Is this because of temperatures and humidities that are too high? Too low? Substrates that are too wet? Too dry? Probably the crowded conditions in which most pets are kept are partially to blame, as is the reliance on fresh water by most keepers. Because hermits are cheap pets, little veterinary attention has been given to the group and we are not even sure of their major diseases and causes of natural death.

Captive Reproduction

Since the marine hobby has become highly developed during the past decade, more and more hobbyists are trying to captive-breed marine fishes and crustaceans. As far as known, there has been no

If it does not suffer an accident and is kept in good conditions with a proper diet, a land hermit crab should live at least a decade in the terrarium.

Breeding

success yet with land hermit crabs, but there is a potential for at least being able to raise-out the eggs of females captured while carrying eggs. This is done in scientific laboratories on a regular basis, though it is not easy and requires a great deal of space, patience, time, and money. Here is an outline of the technique used to raise larval hermit crabs (of all types) in the laboratory.

Captive-raised

It is not impossible to successfully raise the larval stages of land hermit crabs in the laboratory, starting with a female carrying eggs. Tremendous numbers of eggs may hatch, but only a very few will develop through to the tiny hermits that look for their first snail shells on land a couple of months later. Mortality rates of young are tremendous, of course, as with most marine larvae. Will captive-raised land hermits ever become available? Perhaps, if a market can be found to support the high costs of raising the crabs.

A female carrying eggs (which usually can be easily seen when the crab walks about) is placed in an individual container with natural seawater of the appropriate salinity; the container is aerated to assure it stays clean and fresh. Hatching usually occurs in a few days at most, at which point the tiny (under a quarter of an inch), virtually transparent larvae are picked out with a dropper and removed to bowls for further raising as groups of about a hundred larvae. (Remember, you may have as many as 50,000 larvae from a single female.) The water is kept at a constant temperature (usually 60°F or so) under room light and the larvae are fed newly hatched larvae (nauplii) of brine shrimp as well as tiny marine rotifers and unicellular algae. (All these foods are widely available through specialized marine aquarium dealers.) The water is changed daily before feeding, being careful to lose as few larvae as possible. After a month or so most of the zoea should be entering young crab stages and more easily visible to the naked eye. At this time the food can become a bit larger and the water can be changed every two or three days.

Like any captive-raised marine animal, the price of a single captive-raised land hermit crab would obviously have to be multiples of the price of a wild-caught specimen because rearing is so labor-intensive. However, several companies now regularly produce anemonefishes, gobies, damsels, and some other marine species (including a few reef shrimp) at competitive prices, so perhaps it is not an impossible task.

Conservation

Visitors to the Miami area or the Florida Keys can encounter land hermits, *Coenobita clypeatus,* when they poke around under dead palm fronds during the day or as they walk the beaches or woods near beaches at night. The crabs are easy to catch and interesting

Any attempt to raise land hermit crabs in the aquarium will require the proper foods. One of the staples is the tiny larvae of brine shrimp, Artemia, *a crustacean found in salty lakes and bays around the world.*

Breeding

and easy to transport, and many end up as captive pets. The well-meaning tourist may think that since a single female land hermit may produce a thousand to 50,000 eggs a year for a decade or more, it certainly can do no harm to take a few crabs home. The fallacy of this line of reasoning is that each female and her mate exist now as adults. They are here because a thousand or more eggs were deposited by another female five or ten years ago.

If each collector who visited Florida took home one larval hermit crab, or even a hundred, they would never be missed. After all, there are literally millions or billions of larvae produced each year. However, if you remove one adult, it may take years for it to be replaced by another adult. When tourists take a few crabs, this loss is multiplied and it is possible to greatly reduce the number of adults in a popular beach area in just a few years. If commercial collectors were allowed to gather crabs for the market, the loss would occur faster and be greater.

Not Throw Away Pets!

Though they are cheap, land hermits should not be thought of as throw away pets. They can live a decade or more and survive well in the most basic of housing. Many are very colorful, and they spend a lot of time in action. Just because they are cheap is no reason to consider them suitable only for children or to be kept for a few weeks and then discarded.

Worse yet, the environment in southern Florida and throughout the tropical areas of the world is getting progressively more hostile for hermit crabs as well as other marine creatures. People build seawalls and separate the sea beach from the woods. Insecticides and herbicides are lethal to crabs. Draining marshes and beach ponds or filling them in to control mosquitoes effectively wipes out crab populations since this transition area is where the young crabs emerge from the sea to start their life on land.

Because of changes in the way island beaches are used by people, land hermit crabs in the Caribbean (this specimen is from the Virgin Islands) are at risk of losing much of their habitat.

There is no question that *Coenobita clypeatus* is less common today in many parts of southern Florida than it was in the past, and commercial collecting now is curtailed. This species still is abundant on many islands of the Caribbean, however, and still is collected by the tens of thousands. As long as the collecting is spread over the whole range of the species, there probably is no problem, but if collectors concentrate on a few local populations, the crabs will disappear after a few years. There are tens of millions of crabs in the Caribbean, but we do not yet understand how many crabs are necessary to support a local population. If mating, for instance, generally occurs during the gigantic congregations when shells are traded, then perhaps reducing the number of crabs so such congregations no longer occur may stop reproduction and lead to all the local crabs dying out in a decade or two.

Throughout the tropics land hermit crabs are under stress from changes in the coastal environment and from being used locally as fishing bait, food, and (in the case of Coconut Crabs) a source of oil. They are important and colorful scavengers essential in the ecology of tropical seashores, and their loss could be devastating in the long run.

Breeding

Quick & Easy Hermit Crab Care

Species of Land Hermits

Hermit crabs are very specialized crustaceans that, contrary to their name, are a bit more closely related to the lobsters than to the blue crabs used as food. They belong to a group known as Anomura, sometimes called "half crabs." Also in the Anomura are the porcelain crabs often seen living in anemones in large marine aquaria and the spiny lithodids or king crabs of cold waters. All hermit crabs belong to the superfamily Paguroidea, and most of the ones found in the aquarium or terrarium belong to the families Coenobitidae, Diogenidae, and Paguridae. Hermit crabs are recognized by their general shape, usually with a pair of claws (chelae) at the ends of the first pair of legs, long antennae, eyes on fairly long stalks, and a soft abdomen that is asymmetrical in shape, with reduced leg-like appendages compared to a regular shrimp or crab. Except for the Coconut Crab, hermit crabs must hide the abdomen in a shell or a worm tube for protection. Some hermits that live in worm tubes are sedentary, using long bristles on the antennae and mouthparts to filter small particles from the water. Most hermit crabs, however, are active scavengers that may occur in tremendous numbers in favorable habitats, both in the sea and on land and from pole to pole.

Aquatic Hermits

Many marine hobbyists keep hermit crabs in their aquaria as colorful scavengers. Most of these are species of the genera *Paguristes, Calcinus, Clibanarius,* and *Dardanus,* all of which have very colorful species. None of these hermit crabs can be adapted to terrestrial conditions, however, so don't even try.

Of the many hundred species of hermit crabs known to science, relatively few are not found on coral reefs, in the deep sea, or along coastal brackish and fully salt shores. One species is known to live in fully freshwater ponds on the island of Vanuatu (formerly New Hebrides) in the southern Pacific, but overall hermit crabs are strictly marine and not likely to be found above the waterline unless stranded temporarily between tides, pulling into their snail shells to conserve moisture. Land hermit crabs are a great exception to the general rule.

Land Hermits

The few species of terrestrial hermit crabs all belong to the single family Coenobitidae and to just two genera, *Birgus* and *Coenobita.* There are about a dozen species of *Coenobita,* the familiar land hermit crabs, but they are very difficult to distinguish without technical literature and dead specimens. The following is just an attempt to mention a few of the better-known species and give an idea of their range and some recognition characters. Unfortunately, few of these species currently are imported for the terrarium hobby, though it is suspected that most would do well.

Coconut Crabs

The genus *Birgus* is represented by a single species, the Coconut or Robber Crab, *Birgus latro.* This large (to at least six pounds) land-dwelling and climbing hermit is found near coastlines from eastern Africa to the southwestern Pacific, excluding (perhaps because of long-term human predation) the northern part of the Indian Ocean and western Malaysia but extending north into the Ryukyu Islands of Japan. These very active, mostly nocturnal hermit crabs are unique in the group in having a large, symmetrical abdomen covered with hard, chitinous plates. The body (cephalothorax) is very wide, almost oval, and often rough and wrinkled. The claws (pincers) are large and very strong, the left usually a bit larger than

The large size and brightly ringed eyes, as well as the fact that many carry anemones, make the species of Dardanus *popular in marine aquaria.*

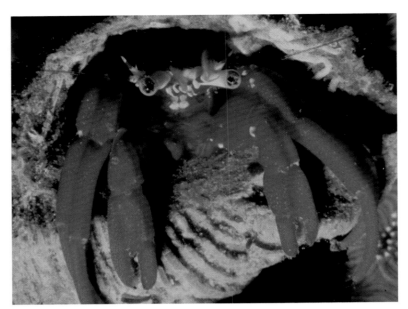

There are few fishes that can compete with the Caribbean Pagurestes
cadenati *when it comes to bright colors. This reef species is one of the most
popular marine hermit crabs.*

the right. Unlike other land hermits, a long rostrum projects
between the eyes. Color varies from bright reddish brown with
white claws to nearly all black. When the larvae emerge from the
ocean (like other land hermits, the female lays her eggs in the sea)
they inhabit shells for a short period, but eventually they become
hard enough to live without that extra protection. Coconut Crabs
are notorious as scavengers that will feed on large dead and dying
animals and also are able to pierce the eyes of a coconut to gain
access to the meat within. They build large burrows in protected
areas and often line them with fiber from coconut husks. Because of
the large amount of oil that develops in their abdomens, humans
prey upon them wherever they occur, and they have become rare in
many areas where formerly abundant. Large specimens may be
dangerous to handle because of the strength of their claws.

True Land Hermits
Coenobita includes the true or familiar land hermit crabs found on

tropical beaches around the world. Unlike the Coconut Crab, the cephalothorax is flattened at the sides (compressed), narrowing toward the eyes, and the first pair of legs (chelipeds) tend to be strongly flattened on the inside so when the crab pulls back into its shell the front legs fit smoothly against the sides of the body. The abdomen is asymmetrical, curved to fit into a shell, and covered with a thin skin that serves as an extra air-exchange surface to aid the gills. Most species are purplish to brownish, with strongly compressed eyestalks and dark brown or reddish brown eyes.

Species are hard to distinguish when alive (and sometimes when preserved), identification often depending on details of how the segments of the legs are proportioned. In most areas of the Indo-Pacific four species are dominant and likely to be found along almost any coastline. A single species occurs in the Caribbean, one is virtually restricted to the Red Sea, and another species is found on the tropical shores of Pacific America. Other species are more rarely observed and even more poorly understood by scientists.

Legends?

Coconut Crabs, because of their large size and edibility, have long attracted human attention, but the species still is not well-studied scientifically. Legends have grown up around this crab, including its ability to cut coconuts off the tree instead of waiting for nuts to drop. It certainly can cut through the husk of a nut and then the eyes of a coconut shell to get to the meat, but it does this more by tearing away small fibers than just slicing through the husk. In World War II, Coconut Crabs were feared by soldiers dug into tropical beaches during battles because they were said to come out at night and feed on dead—and dying—soldiers, an unlikely occurrence. Regardless, Coconut Crabs now are rare in many areas because of persecution by man.

The Caribbean Land Hermit Crab, *Coenobita clypeatus,* is found on most of the islands of the Caribbean from the Bahamas to Trinidad, as well as on the coasts of Venezuela and Colombia plus southern Florida; Bermuda also is home to this species. The left pincer is much larger and heavier than the right and usually bright purple. The third left leg has the two outermost segments extremely broad and flattened. In most larger adults (especially those near molting) the legs are dark reddish brown; younger specimens and those freshly molted may have bright red legs; many individuals have strong purple tints on most of the legs. The eyestalks are strongly flattened and usually reddish, the eyes round and rather small. Large adults have a cephalothorax at least 2 inches long. This is the common species in pet shops, where it usually is represented by young and subadult specimens.

Coenobita clypeatus, the Caribbean Land Hermit, is the only species most hobbyists will ever see. It also is the easiest to keep.

Quick & Easy Hermit Crab Care

The sharply edged body, rather small eyes, and widely expanded legs of the Caribbean Land Hermit are features found in several other species.

Eastern Pacific Land Hermits, *Coenobita compressus,* are found abundantly from the Gulf of California and Baja, Mexico, to the Gulf of Peru. Specimens tend to be a bit paler than the Caribbean species (yellowish to creamy tan or grayish brown), with weaker color highlights (never bright purple) on the claws and walking legs. Typically the last segment of the walking legs is darker than the other segments. The third left leg is not as extremely flattened as in

Don't Collect Your Own

When on vacation in the Caribbean it is sorely tempting to pick up a land hermit or two from a local beach and stick them in a plastic jar or bag for a quick trip back home in your luggage. Be aware that almost all Caribbean areas have strict laws about removing animals from their shores, and the US Customs will not be thrilled if you lie about bringing home living animals. Fines and confiscation of your crabs may await. It is better and cheaper to just purchase crabs at your pet shop.

the Caribbean Land Hermit and does not curve around the large claw quite as well to fill the opening of the shell. The eyes are rather large and compressed. Its natural history and keeping conditions are much like the Caribbean species, except it needs full salt water for drinking and to carry over the gills, not using fresh water well. When specimens appear in the shops, they usually are imported from Ecuador and may be called Ecuadorian Land Hermits. Keep an eye out for this crab at your dealer, as it may be sold mixed with Caribbean Land Hermits.

The Crying Land Hermit Crab, *Coenobita rugosus,* is generally common from the East African coast to the islands of the southwestern Pacific. This is one of the land hermit species with a row of closely spaced spines or pegs along the upper inner surface of the left pincer, a structure called a stridulatory ridge. The crab rubs this row of spines with the other legs or against the body to produce a relatively loud, crying call. In this species the next to last segment of the third left leg is strongly flattened and has a sharp ridge along the upper edge. This tends to be a brownish to chocolate-colored land hermit with just weak purplish highlights.

Strawberry Land Hermit Crabs, *Coenobita perlatus,* also have a stridulatory ridge on the left pincer, but the next to last segment of the third left leg is less flattened than in the Crying Land Hermit and lacks the strong ridge. Additionally, this is one of the most colorful of the crabs, many adults being bright orange-red from the eyestalks over the body and through the legs. Though found from Tanzania to the southwestern Pacific, it usually is thought of as the common Australian land hermit. Occasional specimens reach pet shops and can be treated much like the Caribbean species.

Red Sea Land Hermits, *Coenobita scaevola,* are similar in structure to the Crying Land Hermit, with a stridulatory ridge on the left claw. Unlike that species, however, the color tends to be quite pale, often cream, and there is a large tuft of hair-like setae at the lower

Quick & Easy Hermit Crab Care

Though some are brown, many Strawberry Land Hermits, Coenobita perlatus, *are bright red on all their legs, making them very desirable as pets.*

front edge of the segment just before the claw of the right leg. Virtually restricted to the Red Sea, rarely being found along the eastern African coast to Somalia and perhaps Kenya, it is the only species of land hermit typically found in the Red Sea.

Keep Your Eyes Open

Countries on the Red Sea export a large number of fishes and other marine invertebrates to the aquarium hobby, so it should be expected that some Red Sea Land Hermits might occasionally be shipped. Keep your eyes open for this crab in shops that handle large numbers of other Red Sea specimens. Look for the stridulatory ridge and the large hair tuft.

The Round-eyed Land Hermit Crab, *Coenobita brevimanus,* looks at first glance much like the Caribbean Land Hermit and formerly was confused with that species. Unlike other common land hermits, the eyestalks are not strongly compressed, being more cylindrical. The third left leg is not as flattened as in the Caribbean crab, but

Not all land hermits are brightly colored. This specimen from the Timor Sea, perhaps Coenobita cavipes, *is grayish brown. Notice the very large eyes.*

admittedly the colors may be very similar, with a bright purple left pincer and strong purplish tints on the rest of the legs. Like the other common land hermits, it is found from the eastern African coast to islands of the southwestern Pacific.

Brown Land Hermits, *Coenobita cavipes,* may be common from East Africa to the western Pacific, though apparently absent from the small islands of the southern Pacific. Structurally this species in unremarkable, with a strongly flattened next to last segment of the third left leg that has a strong ridge at the outer edge. There is no stridulatory ridge as in the similar Crying Land Hermit, and purple tints are weak or absent on the claws and legs, which tend to be more or less solid chocolate to dark brown. The body often is spotted with brown and white rather than striped or uniform as in most land hermits.

It is unfortunate that more species of land hermits are not readily available for interested hobbyists. Because only the Caribbean Land Hermit is seen in most pet shops and is sold at such low prices, keeping land hermits has not developed into a hobby appealing to more advanced study, land hermits being considered pets for children and beginners. These large animals are as varied as many fish groups, often colorful, may be quite personable pets, and deserve more attention from serious hobbyists.

Resources

Classroom Hermits
www2.ttu.edu/thomas/classPet/19
99/HermitCrabs/student.htm
Good teacher's guide to using land
hermits as classroom pets.

Fun Site
www4.tpg.com.au/users/vaness-
ap/hermit.html
Interesting site with plenty of
downloadable goodies.

Hermit Crab Association
www.hermit-crabs.com
A great site with loads of accurate
information on land and marine
hermits—start with this one.

Hermit Crab Supplies
www.seashellshop.com/hermit-
crabs.html
A commercial site with much specialized and useful equipment as
well as some care information.

Hermit Webring
k.webring.com/hub?ring=hermie
A webring leading to a variety of
sites on land hermit crabs.

Land Hermit Message Center
www.landhermitcrabs.com/
Useful site for posting your ques-
tions and getting answers from
other keepers.

Seychelles Hermits
www.geocities.com/rainforest/cano
py/5280/coenobit.htm
Illustrated and informative site on
the land hermits of the Seychelle
Islands, Indian Ocean.

Index

Photo Credits

Dr. H. R. Axelrod: 31
P. Bartley: 34
C. Church: 56
I. Francais: 3, 11, 21, 25
U. E. Friese: 53
K. Gillett: 61
M. Gilroy: 1, 4, 8, 9, 15, 16, 17, 26, 27, 28, 29, 30, 35, 39, 40, 41, 45, 47, 52, 58

R. Hunziker: 49
K. Lucas: 51
G. Moore: 18, 19, 52
A. Norman: 55
J. Ronay: 5
Z. Takacs: 6, 7, 62
M. Walls: 13, 22, 23, 37, 42, 43, 44, 59

Quick and Easy Hermit Crab Care